YELLOWSTONE GHOST STORIES

SHELLIE HERZOG LARIOS

RIVERBEND
PUBLISHING

Front cover photo: Old Faithful Inn

Riverbend Publishing
P.O. Box 5833
Helena, MT 59604
Toll-free: 1-866-787-2363
www.riverbendpublishing.com

Contents

DEDICATION

TO my Dad who introduced me to
Yellowstone and took us every year.

TO my Mom whose sewing and
financial skills made it possible for us to go.

TO my sisters Carol and Becky and brother Max
who helped create the fondest of memories.

ACKNOWLEDGMENTS

Those who are crazy enough to take on the task of writing a book realize only too soon its snowballing effect and recognize the gratitude owed to so many.

First, I acknowledge my family with great love and appreciation. I thank Larry, my husband who tirelessly read stories as they were rewritten countless times, and I thank my great kids, Marc and Letitia, who forfeited vacations to places of their choice so we could take innumerable trips to Yellowstone and gather more information. Thanks especially for their individual and creative contributions to this book.

Thanks to my sister Merrillyn who dotted my i's and crossed my t's; to family and friends who read my stories and gave comments and confidence; to Becky and kids, especially Martin who presented my stories to his school class. Thank you to Carol who cuts out everything she ever sees in the newspaper or magazines about Yellowstone; and to my sister Letitia May. Thanks to Paul J. for his encouragement and keen eye, and to Peggie my soul sister who helped me track down the spirits, especially Mattie's.

Acknowledgment goes to all of those associated with the park, both in and out of park uniform, for sharing their stories and experiences. A special thanks to Craig and Pam at the Yellowstone Institute who contributed to this book and encouraged me. A warm acknowledgment to Aubrey L. Haines, who was the final authority on historical questions that were beyond my realm.

And last but certainly not least: I thank Lee H. Whittlesey, J.D., historical archivist and all-around good guy, who at first was justifiably leery of me and my plan to put what he calls "perpetuating Yellowstone baloney" on paper. Later, realizing my commitment to keeping fact and fiction separate, he fearlessly siphoned through my stories to make sure the historical content they did have was, in fact, accurate. In the end he even helped me chase down a ghost or two.

FOREWORD

There is something about the human psyche that causes us to be fascinated by the idea of ghosts, specters, and wraiths. Even to those of us who profess disbelief in such things, anything supernatural generally catches our interest, if only for brief moments.

As a child, my interest in things supernatural and paranormal was stimulated by the many books of Ray Bradbury, L. Frank Baum, and Edward Eager, and of course by the 1950s EC and ACG comic books like *Tales from the Crypt* and *Adventures into the Unknown*. In those wonderful fantasy books, I was introduced to the floating bed sheets, transparent human forms, and other gossamer wraiths that comprise the myriad of disembodied souls we call ghosts.

Later I learned about some of the more classic ghost stories of literature, of which Shakespeare's Hamlet and Macbeth are two of the most famous. Their appearances in 1603 and 1606 make it clear that Elizabethan-era people were fascinated by ghosts if they did not believe in them outright! "I am thy father's spirit...doomed to walk the night," intoned the King from Hamlet, "til the foul crimes—are burnt and purged away."

Throughout history, people in all countries have been fascinated by ghosts, describing or otherwise creating them in poetry, literature, movies, and toys. One of the earliest ghost stories, from around 2000 B.C. and etched on Babylonian clay tablets, tells of the hero Gilgamish and the ghost of his dead friend Enkidu. The Chinese celebrate their "Hungry Ghost Festival" in the seventh moon to appease ghosts, and Japan has a similar celebration called the "Obon Festival." Even the Bible mentions ghosts, per Deuteronomy 18:10-11, Isaiah 8:19, and Samuel 28, although the Good Book generally counsels against "calling them forth." And the Ghosts of Christmas Past, Present, and Future are well known to fans of Charles Dickens.

There are even ghost ships: the *Mary Celeste*, the *Flying Dutchman*, and probably others, destined to ply stormy waters, wraith-like for all eternity, carrying their dead crewmembers and their mysteries. Ghostwriters (no pun intended) tend to mention three kinds of ghosts, and to no one's surprise, they all come from religion: Kindly ghosts from Heaven, evil ghosts from Hell, and the wandering-ones-with-unfinished-business ghosts from purgatory. Why do ghosts lurk? The usual reasons are varied and include unfinished business, lost love, grudges, revenge, and unpaid debts.

In this book author Shellie Larios takes us on a journey into the oldest of national parks, Yellowstone, to find its ghosts. She has tried hard to get the history right, so that you can enjoy the stories and draw your own conclusions. Larios is not trying to present the ghosts as facts, but she does want you to have fun with John Yancey, Ed Wilson, and others in the manner of similar specter-seekers. She even tells us outright about the well-documented origin of the headless bride story from Old Faithful Inn. So determined were ghost hunters to find an Old Faithful Inn ghost story that employees made up a story to appease them. In that spirit, this book is meant to be fun.

And, meanwhile, may things not move about mysteriously in your home or office....

Lee Whittlesey
Archivist, Yellowstone National Park

INTRODUCTION

The thought of ghosts brings to mind unearthly apparitions ascending from dark, misty shadows and grim phantoms who clandestinely float down cold, damp hallways. I've loved ghosts and tales that go bump in the night since childhood. History is brimming with unfinished stories of spirits and specters. In my search of shadows, I have found that Yellowstone is no different. Although I have spent almost 50 years visiting Yellowstone, it has been the last ten years that I have researched and recorded its spirits. You may ask yourself: are these stories true and do I believe in ghosts? In most of the stories, the characters are real and the facts around their lives are referenced in Yellowstone's history books. Like all good legends, however, the ghost part? Well, you'll have to go and make your own decisions. Let's just say that ghost stories told around blazing campfires on dark eerie nights in the woods can be pretty convincing.

AUTHOR'S NOTE

This book was written for pure entertainment and does not claim to be documented reference. Every attempt has been made to give proper credit; however, in the respect of privacy, the author has chosen to use first names of those interviewed. The author further admonishes readers that although most stories are based on facts concerning Yellowstone National Park and the people who lived and worked there, these stories, like most folklore, have been told and retold with the addition of embellishment.

NEXT STOP...GHOST TOWN

Ages ago, one can easily see,
Old Yellowstone Valley went on a spree;
The mountains had risen, the valleys had sunk,
And Old Mother Nature got roaringly drunk.
The Devil, as drunk as the Devil would be,
Slid to the bottom of Cinnabaree.
                    Montana, A State Guide Book

Old Cinnabar can truly be called a ghost town. Why? Because ghosts disappear...and so did Cinnabar! Way before the trailer, camper or "RV" was even thought of, tourists came to Yellowstone National Park by railroad. During this time, the North Entrance to Yellowstone was not only the most accessible entrance but also the most popular way to enter "Wonderland," as it was once called. Every summer people from around the world would ride the Northern Pacific Railroad 51 miles from Livingston, Montana, to the park. The engines climbed almost 700 feet in elevation along the Yellowstone River, through Yankee Jim's Canyon, until they reached the terminus at Cinnabar.

The Cinnabar Station, as well as the town of Cinnabar, was created by the railroad practically overnight in 1883, receiving its name from the bright red stone of Devil's Slide, a prominent, narrow chute on a steep hillside two miles away. But in 1903, Cinnabar was eliminated as quickly as it was created.

Cinnabar only existed because the Northern Pacific wanted it to. The original plans were to lay tracks all the way into Gardiner, Montana, a few miles beyond Cinnabar. The tracks, however, temporarily halted at Cinnabar because of a land squabble with Buckskin Jim, a local man who would not give up his land claim which lay right in the path of the proposed railroad tracks. This dispute was circumvented by building the train station at Cinnabar and then transporting visitors by stagecoach to the park hotel at Mammoth.

In its short twenty years of existence, until the line was eventually extended to Gardiner, Cinnabar was famous for a sixteen-day stint when it served as the "Western White House" for President Theodore Roosevelt. The president visited Gardiner and Yellowstone National Park to dedicate the grand arch at the park's north entrance on April 8, 1903. Arrangements to accommodate the President and his entourage had not been completed at Gardiner, so they set up camp at the Cinnabar railroad station until their April 24 departure.

Secretary William Loeb, Jr., conducted presidential affairs of state from a string of Pullman and parlor cars while couriers commuted to President Roosevelt as he traveled through Yellowstone. During those sixteen days an official of the Associated Press was heard to say, "Well, this blooming town will be wiped off the map when we leave." He didn't know how right he actually was: nine days after the president left, Cinnabar was a virtual ghost town with only the shells of a few buildings left behind as a testament of its brief grandeur. When the train depot at Gardiner was completed, Cinnabar disappeared into the sagebrush.

Today the town isn't even a shadowy semblance of its former self. Its dusty streets are gone. All that is left are the scars made by the old train tracks, long since pulled up. And the houses? Why they are nothing but lonely rows of shallow graves where cellars once held corn and potatoes.

Cinnabar gone, yes, but not forgotten, because some believe that you can sometimes hear a far off whistle of the old locomotive as it approaches. It arrives at Cinnabar just about the same time every year. Coal black in color, it stops and lets off a big burst of steam. It does not have an engineer, nor does it carry a conductor. In fact, it doesn't even let off passengers, but the Ghost Train stops just the same, and as it does, clouds quickly cover the moon and the air chills and fills with the familiar smell of oily, musty, burning coal. Then, as the old engine discharges its final blast of steam into the night, the tired old Ghost Train slowly fades into an ebony-shrouded mist and dissipates into the midnight air.

(Note: The old town site of Cinnabar was annexed into Yellowstone National Park as a part of the "Gardiner Game Ranch" addition in 1932.)

OF MAMMOTH SPIRITS

Have you ever felt something strange for just a moment, and then suddenly it was gone? It may have been a ghost! You see, spirits live in many different dimensions that run parallel to ours. Normally, these dimensions do not ever connect with us, but on occasion they do. Think of a dimension as being a radio frequency. Imagine what happens when one of these dimensions or frequencies fluctuates and becomes close to or even bumps into ours. That's usually when a ghost emerges. It may happen once...randomly...or repeatedly. Thus for a period of time, the ghost becomes part of our world.

When a dimension becomes matched perfectly with our dimension, the spirit or spirits can become beings. But this happens very rarely. Usually the match is much less perfect and the specters appear in transparent forms. More often, there is even a lesser match and the ghost may only show a "sign of presence." This can be a light, sound, smell, touch, chill, or a combination. Because these "signs" are so common, we don't even think of them as being spirits making contact. "Of Mammoth Spirits" is not one story but a collection of experiences from park visitors and employees who have seen, heard, touched, and yes, even smelled the spirits of Yellowstone.

SEEING A LIGHT

For those whose lives have been lit by love, it really isn't hard to imagine "holding a torch" for someone. But how long does one hold this torch? For Ed Wilson, the answer is forever. It's thought Wilson came to Yellowstone in 1885 and worked as a "mountaineer assistant." Soon he became an Army scout, a position he took very seriously. If there were soldiers at the fort who didn't like him, it was because he didn't hesitate to report them if he caught them poaching in the park. There was also a dark side to Ed Wilson, which added to his unpopularity. He spoke of the mysterious and the unseen, and he preferred to travel alone. He nearly always traveled at night, and he would scout in the darkest and fiercest storms.

In 1891 Wilson fell in love with Mary Rosetta Henderson, the youngest daughter of G. L. Henderson, a prominent part of Yellowstone's history. But Mary Rose didn't return Wilson's affections. Being in his late thirties, he must have seemed ancient. Mary had the pick of any young soldier and had no doubt heard the strange stories about Wilson. It soon became obvious he had no chance of winning Mary Rose's hand, and on July 27 he walked up the hill in back of Mammoth Village and poisoned himself. No one knew he left; no one saw him go. When it finally became obvious he was missing, a search was initiated. A year passed before his scantily clothed skeleton was found on the hill where he took his life. There, next to his remains, lay an empty bottle of morphine.

Now, more than a century later, there is a faint light that many people have seen on the top of the hill above the Mammoth Hot Springs Village. Both employees and visitors have seen it. It's not there every night, but sometimes, when there is no moon and the black sky is full of stars, Wilson's dimension bumps into ours. The light on the hill is where Ed Wilson sat and decided, with a heavy heart, that it would be impossible to live without the beautiful Mary Rose.

HEARING GHOSTS OF ARMIES PAST

In 1872 Yellowstone was designated the world's first national park. But this wasn't enough. With no funds allocated for protection, the park was still at the mercy of poachers and souvenir hunters. Finally, in 1886, Captain Moses Harris and a troop of fifty soldiers were sent from Fort Custer and assigned national park duty. The soldiers arrived in Yellowstone late that summer and set up Camp Sheridan at the foot of Capital Hill at Mammoth. This was to be only a temporary arrangement, but it ended up spanning more than thirty years. With this assignment, Captain Harris became the first "military" superintendent of the park.

In 1890 Congress designated funds for a permanent post at Yellowstone. By this time, Camp Sheridan had grown considerably and was replaced by Fort Yellowstone. The fort was enlarged several times and eventually four troops were assigned to it. But the fort had its share of sadness. Soldiers, civilians, and family members died in Yellowstone and many were buried in the Fort Yellowstone Army Cemetery. In 1916 the National Park Service was created, bringing a bittersweet end to the Army's control.

At sunset on July 4, 1916, the old garrison cannon, perched atop Capitol Hill, was fired for what was probably the last time. The United States Army then vacated the park, leaving only its ghosts behind. Strangely enough, the Army soon came and got them too. The very next year, the remains of all military personnel buried in the Fort Yellowstone Army Cemetery were mysteriously dug up and transferred to the military cemetery that what was then called Custer's Battlefield, in southeastern Montana. Today the Mammoth horse corrals share a hillside with the old Fort Yellowstone graveyard. On occasions, late in the evening, voices can be heard coming from the direction of the old fenced-in graves. The voices are calling for their fathers and husbands and friends who were taken and will never return.

THE HOUSE THAT HIRAM HAUNTS

Hiram Martin Chittenden is considered to be one of Yellowstone's most remarkable figures. Assigned to the Army Corps of Engineers, he spent two tours of duty in Yellowstone. In 1891, as a lieutenant, he was placed in direct charge of the construction and maintenance of roads and bridges. Like many, he fell under Yellowstone's magical spell. On his second tour of duty in 1899, he was assigned the post of engineer officer. Chittenden was delighted to be back in

Yellowstone. This was his favorite station and the place where he and his family were the happiest. Each spring they looked forward to returning to clean air and spectacular scenery.

In 1902, given a bigger budget, Chittenden turned his attention to buildings and offices, including a new mess house and a brand new home for himself. Chittenden's house was built just east of the Mammoth Hot Springs Hotel. Being of wood construction, the house was simple in design and Chittenden loved it. He spent many hours at his desk reading, writing, and pondering the future of Yellowstone while enjoying his favorite cigars.

After the 1905 season, Chittenden returned to his winter home in Sioux City and was later stationed in the northwest. He died in 1917, never returning to Yellowstone, at least not alive. Since his death, however, he has returned to his beloved Yellowstone and to his home many times.

The Chittenden home is now occupied by the offices of the Yellowstone Association and the Yellowstone Institute. For a while Chittenden showed no signs of his presence. Recently, however, he has become very obvious. He often fiddles with computers in the office and flickers the lights. The staff sometimes finds that he randomly opens and closes doors. One staff member related that late one evening when he returned to the building to pick up something he had left, as he ascended the stairs the office door opened for him, an inviting gesture on Hiram's part.

The most conclusive evidence of Hiram's presence is the aroma of his cigar. The smell permeates his old house, especially upstairs in the Yellowstone Institute offices which were once the bedrooms. The smell ordinarily would not cause attention, but smoking in public buildings has been prohibited for many years.

What a perfect place for Hiram to haunt, but why has he come back? Before he died, Chittenden confided that he only regretted not accomplishing more while posted in Yellowstone. Now he returns as a seasoned mentor...a guardian spirit for those who seek his inspiration and guidance. The poet Henry Wordsworth Longfellow said it best when he wrote, "All Houses in which men have lived and died are Haunted Houses: Through the open doors the harmless phantoms on their errands glide with feet that make no sound upon the floors."

CHILLS AT THE HAMILTON STORE

The Hamilton Store holds a prominent place in Mammoth's history. As one of the oldest buildings in the village, it holds within its walls more than one hundred years of spirits.

The specter in this story was discovered almost two decades ago and quite by accident, but it still remains quite active. While I was researching another story in the West Thumb area, an employee working at the Hamilton Store in Grant Village shared an experience his friend had while she was working at the Hamilton Store in Mammoth.

It was the summer of 1983 and this particular employee had been working as a clerk for most of the season. One evening, just after closing, she went upstairs to the storage room to get some items to restock the shelves. Suddenly she heard quick, strong, footsteps and the rustling of a long dress and petticoats. The footsteps came up the stairs and down an aisle closer to her. Just as the footsteps stopped, a hand touched her, but as she turned...no one was there. She kept the experience to herself until overhearing another employee telling of a similar encounter. Both employees shared their experiences with each other and agreed they had been visited by the same spirit. It started with footsteps up the stairs, then the rustling of a long skirt and petticoats, and finally the touch of a hand.

Who is the spirit that visits the upstairs storage room? Why does it come and what does it want? The strong footsteps suggest an adult, and the rustling of a dress with petticoats makes it a woman from the late 1800s when long dresses were in fashion. But who? There are four likely candidates: G. L. Henderson's four daughters.

In the spring of 1882, Henderson, a widower, came to the park with his son and four daughters. Barbara G. Henderson, or "Lillie" as she was known by her family, was appointed postmistress of the park in July. In 1896, about the same time the store was built, Lillie married Alex Lyall. He was a building contractor and probably played an active role in the building of the store, along with Lillie's father.

Alex and Lillie ran the store and later entered into a partnership with Lillie's sister Jennie Henderson Ash to operate other stores at various points in the park. Because the store was part of the Henderson/Lyall enterprise and because Henderson had four daughters, our spirit could really be any one of them. But our instincts tell us it is Lillie who busily sachets through the store, putting things in place, dusting, and looking over shoulders of visitors who also hear the footsteps and petticoats and feel her touch, only to turn and see no one. Yes, it's Lillie, the original storekeeper, who is greeting visitors and following the staff to make sure that everything in her store is in its proper place.

PHANTOM ON THE FLOORS

Ghost stories start out as incidents related to a friend or sightings of some kind shared with others. Sometimes the tales remind us of a similar event we've experienced, and these experiences, seasoned with a little history and research, often mysteriously evolve into a ghost story. The spirit(s) in the following story haven't been thoroughly investigated, but there's enough information to make one wonder.

In July 1996, my family and I visited Yellowstone. I was doing some research in the library at Mammoth. We were excited because it was the first time we had stayed at the Mammoth Hot Springs Hotel. We were given keys to a room on the second floor and directed to the stately staircase. When we reached our room the door would not open, so I returned to the front desk for help. I explained the problem to the tall, slender, desk clerk from Florida. She turned to another woman behind the desk and announced, "Looks like we have another door that won't open." She gave me a forced smile and said she was told that the hotel was so old the doors just got stuck. But she didn't sound convincing so I asked, "Do you think its something else?"

She said no more and handed me the key to another room. When I got to the floor where my family was waiting, I led them down the hall to our new room and told them what had just happened. Needless to say, we set our intended research aside and went ghost hunting at the Mammoth Hotel.

My daughter and I started talking with the housekeeping staff. We were told that just the week before someone was cleaning a room on the fourth floor and went into the hallway to grab some supplies. In that split second, the room door swung shut and would not open. The housekeeper started to panic. Realizing the room next to it had a door that connected the two rooms, she went through it and entered the room she had been working in. To her shock, a dresser was now blocking the door. This frightened her. She knew that no one had entered that room and moved the dresser. She ran out and found another housekeeper but when they returned to the room, the dresser was back in its original place and the door was wide open.

Next we checked with one of the housekeeping supervisors who had worked there for more than a decade. She, too, had heard stories but had never seen anything. She did say, however, that although the phantom's presence has been felt throughout the old hotel, most of the activity seemed to be on the fourth floor. A hotel maintenance man told us that when he first arrived on the job, someone told him of a ghost on the fourth floor. Though he had never seen it firsthand, he could attest to the fact that within seconds doors were often mysteriously locked and unlocked with no human hand or key. He also said that furniture was mysteriously moved to different places throughout the hotel, especially the furniture in storage. There was never an explanation. We questioned others, but most were reluctant to share stories, probably because we were strangers.

After the interviews, our next step was to research the hotel's history. We found that the current hotel was built in 1936 but it was not the first hotel on the site. In 1883 construction started on a hotel. It took about thee years to complete and was quite a grand structure. Nonetheless, the hotel had to be remodeled and enlarged many times over the years to keep up with the growing number of seasonal visitors. Finally in 1936, the original hotel was completely demolished except for the north wing, which had been built in 1911. In 1937 the beautiful map room, present lobby, and gift shop were added, transforming it into the hotel it is today.

The hotel's construction was interesting, but still the question remained. Who is the ghost? Actually it could be anyone from staff members to builders to guests. But spirits often haunt places they were born in, places they dearly loved, or places where they died. Knowing this, we found two prime candidates.

The first is Mary J. Foster. Mary died in 1883 at the age of 33. She was originally from Madison County, North Carolina. Little else is known about her. She was probably an employee of the hotel or of Haynes Photo, and she was the first person buried at the little Mammoth Cemetery on the summit north of the hotel. She was buried on June 10, 1883. We don't know the cause of death. It would be interesting to know if her death was connected with the hotel and its construction, since she died the same year that construction started. Maybe after Mary's death, she chose to take up her eternal residence in the beautiful new Mammoth Hotel.

A second possibility (and our choice) is Emily Sivert. She was the youngest daughter of Chaplain H. A. Sivert, of the 9th U.S. Calvary. We don't know her age or the cause of death. We do know she died August 13, 1903, in the hotel. Emily was buried on August 14 at the Fort Yellowstone Army Cemetery. Maybe Emily is playing jokes in the hotel. Maybe she's teasing guests and staff.

Of course, the spirit could be someone we don't know anything about. But we do know that mysterious things continue to happen at the Mammoth Hotel.

RIVER STYX

G. L. Henderson, dubbed the godfather of Yellowstone, was one of the park's original promoters. He was an early-day park warden, transportation operator, guide, hotelier, and storekeeper. He is given credit for naming many park features. We're not sure if all of the names originate with him or if he passed on some common names already in use. His strong interest in mythology and his use of mythological names leads us to believe he probably named many features because they still hold those names today.

Henderson took many tourists into the upper hot spring terraces of Mammoth. One particularly favorite place was the River Styx and the Devil's Kitchen. Although accessible by the public, few know where it is. If you know anything about Greek mythology, you know there is good reason to be leery of the River Styx.

Yellowstone's River Styx is a hot water creek that originates in the upper Mammoth Hot Spring Terraces and disappears underground. In Greek mythology the River Styx is believed to be the principle and most famous river of Hades. It winds around the underworld nine times, forming the border of Hades and separating the world of the living from the world of the dead. The word Styx comes from the Greek word *stygian* which means hate, therefore the river could be appropriately called the river of hate. This is somewhat intriguing because there are also caves called Stygian located near the Yellowstone stream. These caves have had a long history of emitting poisonous gases that are deadly to birds, insects, and some small animals.

The mythical belief is that the River Styx can only be crossed by the dead. Upon one's death, the spirit departs its mortal body and begins its first journey to the underworld. The dead souls congregate near or on the river's shore. Each wicked soul seeks his or her passage from Charon (Caron), the old ferryman who transports them across the river and takes them to Hades. Only those souls who can afford Charon's fees are ferried across. For this reason, the dead must always be buried with a coin (called an obol) in their mouths. Those who cannot pay are doomed to haunt the riverbanks through eternity.

In the early years of Yellowstone National Park, the River Styx and the Stygian Caves, along with what was called the Devil's Kitchen, were often frequented by tourists. They were part of Henderson's Mammoth Hot Spring tour and cited in his 1885 and 1888 guidebooks called *Yellowstone Park Manual and Guide.* He even built a ladder which took countless tourists down into Devil's Kitchen cave for more than five decades, until 1939. After it was discovered that the gases of the Kitchen, along with the Stygian Caves, were actually lethal, that part of the tour was closed. Even today small animals and birds sometimes die from carbon monoxide that accumulates in low areas.

So as sure as the mysterious old River Styx still flows underneath the earth in the upper terrace, Charon, the old ferryman, still picks up those dead souls willing to pay and carries them to their endless inferno.

THE SENTINEL OF YELLOWSTONE

Most Yellowstone bears never become famous. Aside from a few known and named by locals and park personnel, bears live very anonymous lives. However, a story is told of a bear named Wahb. The word Wahb is the Shoshone word for white bear. Wahb's story, *The Biography of a Grizzly* by Ernest Thompson Seton, was first printed in 1899 and has since become a classic. Wahb fulfills the destiny of a great silver-tipped grizzly in Yellowstone, and thus we learn of his spirit.

Wahb was born in the mountains east of Yellowstone National Park. There he played with his brothers without care until one day he watched as his family was destroyed by the gunfire of a nearby cattle rancher. Now orphaned, he spent his days alone in the wilderness of northwestern Wyoming. As Wahb grew, he collected wounds and wisdom from man and animal. He learned to trust only his instincts. Growing into a mighty bear, he fought a life-long battle against his enemies, and in maturity he truly ruled his territory. Wahb could toss large pine trees for yards and wipe out enemies with one quick swing of his paw. Everyone and everything that knew him wisely kept their distance.

One summer Wahb learned of a safe haven where bears were provided with food every day. Rumors were that in this special park, humans brought food to the bears. This was how Yellowstone's hotels disposed of their garbage in the early years. After finding out about Yellowstone's generosity, and its laws which protected all wild animals within its boundaries, Wahb set out to find this sanctuary. He spent most of the summer there and enjoyed it so much that he made it his annual summer retreat. This, along with a warm spring nearby where he soaked his tired bones, became his ritual.

Many summers soon passed, and being in his prime, Wahb was feared as the most powerful beast in Yellowstone. His only two enemies were a pesky, young, roach-back grizzly from the nearby Bitterroot Range and his own advancing age. The roach-back may have been younger but Wahb was still smarter and more powerful, which gave him the edge as his little nemesis was still very frightened of him. Wahb's second enemy, age, was slowly stripping him of his energy and his sight. Using his keen smell, Wahb knew when the little roach-back was not too far away and he strived to stay one step ahead.

Near the end, Father Time eventually caught up with old Wahb. He could still frighten the little roach-back grizzly by merely making his presence known in the area, but he knew in his heart that it would only be a matter of time. His failing health prompted him to begin questioning his invincibility. He knew it would be madness to battle the young bear. Weeks went by and his pains grew worse. Wahb now hobbled along the hillsides where he had once leaped.

One spring on his way to the park, the west wind brought to Wahb the odor of Death Gulch, the sour-smelling valley where everything, including the air, was dead. This odor, which once sickened and disgusted him, now called to him, saying, "Come and find peace." As Wahb stood at the entrance of the gulch, he saw other peaceful victims lying lifelessly near a spring. He swung his head from side to side and found it easy to breathe the strange aroma of pungent death. That spring day Wahb laid down and in Seton's words:

"Far below him, to the right and to the left and on and on as far as the eye could reach, was the great kingdom that once had been his; where he had lived for years in the glory of his strength; where none had dared to meet him face to face. But Wahb had no thought of its beauty; he only knew that it was a good land to live in; that it had been his, but now it was gone, for his strength was gone, and he was flying to seek a place where he could rest and be at peace....A rush of his ancient courage surged in the grizzly's rugged breast. He turned aside into the little gulch. The deadly vapors entered in, filled his huge chest and tingled in his vast, heroic limbs as he calmly lay down on the rocky herbless floor and as gently went to sleep, as he did that day in his Mother's arms by the Greybull, long ago."

One has only to enter the boundaries of the park to feel the spirit of Wahb, the great silver-tipped grizzly. As others before him, Wahb's ghost now posts himself as sentry outside Death Gulch, located in the northeastern part of the park. Wahb's eternal job is to beckon others who also must pass on. But his ghost is felt by many to be the great spirit of Yellowstone.

Native Americans believe the grizzly bear to be a grandfather who renders power and strength to all. Their stories tell us he is the ruler of the beasts and master of the mountains. This being true, it is only fitting that Yellowstone be protected by Wahb and that his ghost lives there forever.

YANCEY'S GHOST

"Poltergeist" is a German word composed of "poltern," meaning noises or rattle, and "geist," meaning ghost or spirit. Invisible or partly visible, poltergeists interact with and sometimes through animals and young people. Poltergeists play pranks in houses and on families, or in buildings where groups of people gather. These noisy ghosts use furniture and other possessions to get the attention they are seeking. They engage in mischievous pranks, resulting in discomfort and alarm but not fatalities. This is a story of a colorful old character who might just have a true poltergeist personality....

Way up in the northeast corner of Yellowstone, midway between Mammoth and Cooke City, an old and almost forgotten dirt road travels through a beautifully quiet hollow called Pleasant Valley. There, along the west bank of the Yellowstone River, is Yancey's Hole. This spot, along with a few more natural areas, was named for an old southern gentleman named John F. Yancey, popularly referred to by all as "Uncle John." He is noted in history as one of Yellowstone's original squatters, and with a lease from the government, he built and operated a hotel in the park.

It's pretty safe to say that Uncle John came from down Kentucky way. Born in 1826, he was the sixth of ten children. Being a sickly child, he wasn't expected to live long, but ironically he ended up outliving all his siblings.

Yancey's travels started as a child when his family moved to Missouri. When the Civil War started, Yancey took up his musket and fought for the cause he felt was right. When the South lost, he turned to the hills of Nebraska. After chasing the railroad to Salt Lake City and panning for gold in California, Yancey found himself wandering again, and in 1882 he stopped in Yellowstone. In Pleasant Valley he built a station that was a primitive cave-like dwelling made of rock walls and earth roof. It was a crude accommodation, and its main purpose was to serve the local teamsters driving freight wagons to and from the area mines. However, soon the site became a well-established retreat for sports and spirits.

In 1884 Yancey was granted ten acres of Yellowstone land and built a two-story rustic log hotel measuring about 20 x 43 feet. Later a saloon was added and then a barn, some sheds, and a mail station. At this point, Yancey sent out word inviting everyone to visit his Pleasant Valley Hotel, claiming that it was "The Prettiest Place in all of the Rocky Mountains, with excellent Accommodations for Tourists and Travelers."

Many would argue that the only truth in this statement was that it was "The Prettiest Place in all of the Rocky Mountains." The rooms were drafty, the beds had lice, and the food was so bad that complaints were made constantly to Major Pitcher, the park superintendent. The hotel had five small rooms upstairs, each with a single bed, a crate holding a washbowl, a water pitcher, and a piece of a towel. Room numbers were crudely chalked above the doorways, and the extravagant bridal suite was distinguished only by having its own mirror. Even so, Uncle John became genuinely popular and his hotel was a success.

Yancey boasted of good whiskey and rightly so. It was by far the best-tasting stuff around Yellowstone. Swearing it was the real thing straight out of "ole kaintuk," Yancey actually tamed his own recipe of "rotgut" with fermented orange syrup.

Uncle John Yancey was truly an interesting fellow. It was said he was a bone fide frontiersman, but there was something about him that seemed peculiar. His unmistakable southern drawl and refusal to wear any type of blue jeans because their color reminded him of Union Army pants validated his birth in the heart of Dixie and his position as a true soldier in the Confederate Army.

No one really knew why he came to Yellowstone. Maybe he was disheartened by the Civil War and came west to escape and forget. One thing seems for certain: people found him to be an honorable gentleman with an amiable sense of humor. Being somewhat of an eccentric, each and every evening after everyone had retired to their rooms, it was said that lonely old Uncle John would climb up the steep rugged stairs into the dirty attic of his saloon where he would sleep on the cold floor with his two hound dogs. There is no record of a Mrs. Yancey or children at the Pleasant Valley Hotel, but we know that Yancey had three nephews in Montana. Though sociable, it seems Yancey had no close friends.

The Pleasant Valley Hotel hosted the famous as well as the nameless, and Yancey's grand and elite circle of patrons grew to include famous authors, artists, sportsmen, and politicians. He even knew President Theodore Roosevelt. In fact, it was on April 24, 1903, when the president dedicated the cornerstone of the arch at Yellowstone's north entrance, that Yancey caught a cold. The cold quickly turned into pneumonia and Yancey died on May 6. It was said of his passing that "the park lost one of its most colorful characters."

John F. Yancey was buried on Tinker's Hill, just outside the park's boundary at that time. This should have been the end of old Uncle John Yancey, but it certainly wasn't. Three years after his death, his hotel burned to the ground and was never rebuilt. Now nothing is left of old Yancey except a few areas which bear his name. There is no doubt, however, that Uncle John still visits quite often.

With his home gone, Uncle John Yancey's ghost seems to have settled in the Roosevelt Lodge near Pleasant Valley. Employees there frequently experience odd occurrences and blame them on the old man. With his poltergeist soul, his noisy energy makes his presence known. He travels the halls at night, banging on the doors of the staff's quarters with his old tin coffee cup. Employees often keep a radio turned up to get some sleep. Yancey loves to move around items in the lodge kitchen. It's not rare for things which once were lost to turn up later in the strangest places!

Today, Yancey's ghostly presence is especially felt at the Roosevelt corrals. One night Dave, one of the lodge's wranglers, and his friend led their horses to the stable upon returning from a late ride. Dave offered to take care of the saddles and asked his friend to bring the feedbags. When his friend returned with a feedbag, both men were surprised to see that his horse already had a feedbag around its head. It was apparent that neither man had done it, so they blamed Yancey. This frightened the friend and he disappeared. So Dave unhitched his saddle and put it away. Then he turned to take care of the other horse and was startled to see the horse's bare back. The saddle had already been put away.

Why does Yancey's ghost linger around the Roosevelt area? Why did he wait for more than twenty-five years after his death to return? Yancey was buried on Tinker's Hill, which at the time was not inside Yellowstone. Since the National Park Service bought the land surrounding the cemetery, Yancey has returned. He has chosen the Roosevelt Lodge because its operation is familiar to him. The lodge still uses horses and wagons and stagecoaches, so to Yancey, it must feel much like his old hotel. As for the noises? It's the Old Southern Gentleman making sure he is not forgotten.

Yancey isn't spoken of much anymore. But as one of Yellowstone's true pioneers, Yancey's spirit remains. So when you are around the Roosevelt area, perhaps in the lodge or stables, and hear odd noises or see strange and unusual things...and if you are brave enough to investigate but find nothing...remember Old Uncle John Yancey. He was here first!

SPIRITS OF THE BANNOCK

Bannock is the name of an Indian tribe who shared the Snake River plains southwest of Yellowstone with their relatives, the Shoshoni. The Bannock were really nomads. Before they had horses, they traveled on foot in Idaho and parts of Nevada, Utah, and Wyoming. After horses were introduced, their area expanded to include what became Yellowstone National Park and areas further northeast for their annual bison hunts. The Bannock traveled using the same trail for about forty years, from approximately 1838 through the Bannock War of 1878.

"The Bannock Trail," or the "The Great Trail of the Indians" as some call it because of its wide use by many tribes, runs right through Yellowstone. It's undoubtedly an eternal resting place for many of those souls who have left the mortal earth as we know it. The belief that spirits of the dead seek a final place to dwell on earth was and still is a belief shared by most Indian tribes. The common view was that no one owns Mother Earth but only lives on it and shares it during a very short lifetime and then becomes part of it in afterlife. Indians often sought wisdom and strength from spirits, and ancestral spirits were invited into personal lives to provide counsel through life's journey. Because early Native Americans did not believe in heaven, hell, or any other unearthly dwelling for that matter, the tribal elders taught that the souls of the dead remained on earth and became one with the natural habitat. These spiritually perceptive people were accustomed to living among the reflections of their ancestors. They felt close to them and knew their strength as they traveled and camped along the Great Trail. Spiritual leaders often saw and talked to the spirits on the Great Trail, for this is where many were born and many died, and this is where many spirits still linger.

Today you can travel part of the Great Trail in the park. It's a beautiful drive on a well-kept dirt road, the Blacktail Plateau Drive. The drive starts approximately nine southeast of Mammoth off the road to Tower Junction. Along the drive you can almost see the campfires and tepees that once marked the Great Trail. Be sure to drive slowly and get out and take a moment or two to look for the spirits' ghostly reflections in the rocks and hills and feel their inspiring presence in the trees and forests. They are watching over you. Then remember, as you leave this Great Trail of the Indians on your own life's journey, that you too have witnessed the old Bannock spirits blending into the wilderness, perhaps in the cloudy shadows that float across the trail.

IMAGINARY COMPANIONS

Most believers of ghosts and spirits think of them as remnants of the dead that return to haunt, but of course this is only one perspective. You will find the following story somewhat different than the routine. It brings to light spirits from within oneself. For some, these spirits are the most frightening of all. These inner spirits who live with us often quietly wait until we are all alone and most vulnerable. Then they creep into our minds and bodies. These spirits are terrifying because they come from inside, and they are, in essence, the possessors of our deepest and darkest secret demons.

It's said that Yellowstone National Park owes its very existence to three exploring parties who visited between the years of 1869 and 1871. The Yellowstone expedition conducted in 1870, more commonly called the Washburn-Langford-Doan Expedition, was probably the most important and definitely the most famous. For out of it came the notorious story of the birth of the national park idea. It is said that near the end of their trip, as the members sat around a campfire at the junction of the Firehole and Madison rivers, they envisioned the area as a national park for the benefit and enjoyment of all people. The rest, as they say, is history.

The expedition took place in late summer and consisted of eighteen men. Among them was a man named Truman C. Everts. He was an ex-U.S. assessor from Montana, and of all the members on this particular expedition, Everts was the least likely candidate for the trip. In fact, many historians have wondered why, at the age of fifty-four with little wilderness experience and extreme nearsightedness, Everts even considered taking a trip of this proportion.

We know little more about Everts except that he was born in Vermont in 1816, the son of a ship captain, and spent time on his father's ship sailing on the Great Lakes as a cabin boy. At the time of the expedition, Everts was between jobs. He had lost his position as the assessor for the Internal Revenue in the Montana territory and was ready to return to the east coast. So Everts' trip with the Washburn-Langford-Doane party was sort of a vacation...something to do while deciding what to do next. He was quoted as saying that it was the strange and marvelous tales about Yellowstone that had prompted him to go with the expedition in the first place. Unfortunately Everts was to find that his curiosity for this "strange and marvelous" place would almost take his life.

The expedition began on August 17 and for Everts, it seemed doomed from the start. Within a week of departure, Everts became ill and stayed behind at a ranch while the rest of the party traveled on to explore. Everts caught up with them two days later. Soon after, Everts became separated from the party and this time, adding to his plight, he lost his horse, which was a fate worse than death. Without a horse, he had no survival gear, no bedroll, weapon, food, or even the means to make a fire. Everts decided to travel in the direction he thought would allow the rest of the group to find him if they were looking. But because of his lack of experience, he traveled in the wrong direction. After days of walking in the wilderness, he feared he might never be found.

Everts was worn out and on the brink of starvation. His wandering led him to a small lake but he had no way of catching a fish to eat. One night he was treed by a mountain lion. The cold temperatures and his hunger and fear grew worse. As the week passed he grew weaker and his mental state became more impaired. Then imaginary companions started to haunt him.

Everts called the companions "impressions of insanity" and said he was constantly aware of traveling in a dreamland. Or was it a nightmare? He felt that he "possessed a duality of being." He talked to the different beings which he felt came from within himself. They constantly reminded him of his condition and fed his imagination with erratic notions of the most extravagant character.

Everts said he seemed to remain perfectly conscious of the morbid influences and did at times try to shake them, but he found that they often returned with reinforcement. One evening he imagined the blazing eyes of a formidable forest monster spying on him from the dense thicket. Real or not, Everts said he prepared, at any moment, for the monster to make its deadly leap and devour him completely.

Later, while trying to decide whether to search for an escape over the mountains or return to the Yellowstone River and follow it out, Everts said he had strange hallucinations. Friends and readers of his story referred to his condition as insanity. Everts, however, thought it providence that an old friend, whose counsel he often sought, appeared to him in the Yellowstone wilderness and admonished him to return to the river. Everts recounts in his story that his imaginary companion's advice was to, "Go back immediately, as rapidly as [his] strength [would] permit." The apparition explained that there was no food in the mountains and trying to scale the rocks was sheer madness. Everts at first resisted. He felt that the Yellowstone River was too far, but the apparition convinced him that his life depended on his turning around and traveling as fast and as far as possible. Once Everts decided to do so, his imaginary friend stayed close by his side all the next day and was always ready with words of encouragement.

Eventually Everts lost all sense of time. Days and nights came and went, but he remembers only being conscious of the fact that he was starving, yet he felt no hunger. At night, Everts had wonderful dreams of grand restaurants, ones he remembered in New York and Washington. He dreamed of sitting down to tables of rich food, and when he awoke he felt he had spent the entire night eating. When he finally reached the canyon of the river again, Everts was wet and cold. He was in terrible shape and prayed only for sleep and forgetfulness.

We don't know for sure if Everts' prayers for forgetfulness were answered, but we do know that when he was found by "Yellowstone Jack" Baronett near Devil's Cut (or Gut), some fifty miles north of where he became lost, he was inarticulate and irrational. He had been lost in the wilderness for thirty-seven days.

Truman C. Everts lived to tell his story of peril and never once denied the fact that he was visited, perhaps even saved, by imaginary companions.

THE RATTY GHOSTS

"The Ratty Ghosts" may be the only ghost story ever recorded in a National Park Service ranger's report. This unique little story had its own mysterious way of getting into print and almost didn't make it.

When we started researching this book, everyone asked, "Have ya heard the one about the ghosts in the Old Fountain Hotel?" Truth is, it was one of the first stories suggested to us. Strangely enough, everyone knew the story but no one could come up with its origin. Most sources told us that it was somewhere in Aubrey Haines' two-volume book entitled *The Yellowstone Story* but that proved false. After three years of dead ends, we contacted Mr. Haines in hopes he would solve the mystery. He did. It was not in his book or any book. He directed us to the writings of an early Yellowstone ranger and through these writings, the story is finally told.

The Fountain Hotel was built in 1890 for what was at that time an exorbitant price of $100,000. It was built in the Lower Geyser Basin on a tree-covered hill about a quarter mile north of the present Fountain Paint Pots parking area. Today the main road cuts through a portion of that hill and the hotel was just east of the road.

Owned by a private concessionaire, the Yellowstone Park Association, Fountain Hotel was built to pamper the wealthy visitor. It was the largest hotel in the park and its rooms were first occupied during the 1891 season. It succeeded the old Firehole Hotel, which was then burned to the ground.

Upon completion, the Fountain Hotel boasted 143 rooms, steam heat, baths using hot springs water, and electricity. Many rooms had spectacular views of the Fountain Geyser area. If that was not enough, its frequent gala balls allowed gentlemen and lady visitors to unpack their silks and suits for a grand social life.

In 1904 the Old Faithful Inn opened its doors and welcomed guests to a new and unique experience of what some called the largest log building in the world. This development emptied many of the Fountain Hotel rooms. In 1915 the Secretary of the Interior allowed automobiles into the park, and the Fountain Hotel was doomed. Everyone drove the extra seven miles to stay in the Old Faithful Inn and watch the world-famous geyser for which the inn was named. By 1917 the Fountain Hotel was abandoned. Ten years later, after being razed, the hotel's remains were finally burned and the site cleaned up. Rangers and others said it was just as well that the hotel was gone...because it was haunted.

It seems that on one crisp autumn day the hotel's winter-keeper was aroused by the ringing of a service bell connected to one of the hotel rooms. Even though he knew the room was empty, he felt the need to check it out. When he arrived at the room, he found exactly what he knew he would: absolutely nothing. The following day, at precisely the same time, the winter-keeper was again aroused by the same service bell ringing from the same hotel room. Now he knew that not only was that room vacant, but the whole hotel was empty, as the tourist season was over and preparations were being made to close the hotel for the winter. Nevertheless, the winter keeper ventured down the hall to the room. He found it empty.

The next day the bell rang again at the same time, and again the day after that, and so on for days and days. Each day the bell rang at the same time. Each time the winter-keeper went immediately to the room, and each time he was met with the same eerie results. As can be imagined, these kinds of odd, unexplained occurrences would frighten anyone. Finally the poor winter-keeper could stand it no more. He refused to remain in the haunted hotel and fled, vowing never to return. As far as we know, he never did.

A few months after the winter-keeper abandoned the hotel, a park investigation reached an unusual but perhaps more believable conclusion: it was a mouse. Apparently a mouse had built its nest in the walls of the ghostly room. Every evening at the same time the mouse would go out to gather food and do whatever else mice do, and it would crawl through the hotel's walls. As it crawled, it stepped on the bell wire, causing the bell to ring.

The ghostly tale of the call-bell in the Fountain Hotel spread throughout the park and through newspapers across the country. Our version is based on the entries found in a collection of notes by Newell F. Joyner.

LEROY PIPER—LOST FOREVER

During its quarter of a century in operation, the Fountain Hotel was said to be a cut above the rest. As one of the larger hotels and having "the latest of comforts," it catered to the more affluent and wealthy tourists. The hotel boasted a grand social life, and with one of Fort Yellowstone's soldier stations just up the road, it was often filled with dashing young men in uniform who only added to its classic charm.

The hotel had its share of mysteries. This is one of the stories we know, but surely there are more. Though the hotel stood for only a few decades, the Piper mystery has haunted us for more than a century. It's probably one of the most famous Yellowstone stories and still not much is known...except that a guest stepped away from the hotel one evening and utterly vanished.

LeRoy R. Piper came to Yellowstone from St. Mary's, Ohio. He was a bank cashier for the First National Bank of St. Mary's and had a personal worth of approximately $100,000 dollars, a grand sum in those days. He was most likely a man of substance and clout. He wore two diamond rings and his fraternal organization pins. Naturally, the upper-crust Fountain Hotel suited him to a tea.

Piper was on his way to San Francisco to settle his late uncle's estate. Being in the west, he probably felt that a quick trip to the famous park would be the experience of a lifetime and another boost for his social standing.

Piper arrived at the Fountain Hotel on July 29, 1900. He probably arrived by the customary form of transportation: a stagecoach pulled by a team of horses and driven by one of the transportation company's drivers. He and other tourists would have been coming from Mammoth Hot Springs, where tourists usually stayed their first night in the park.

The next day, July 30, it's speculated that Piper and other tourists would have traveled to the Upper Geyser Basin to witness the famous Old Faithful Geyser and other rambunctious geysers shooting their scalding water hundreds of feet into the sky. After spending the day exploring the magnificent sights, Piper may have returned to his room to write to his wife in Ohio. After a brief rest, he would have washed and dressed for supper, and then the distinguished Piper most likely would have descended the staircase promptly on the hour. He'd blend in with the other prominent men, and wearing his fine blue suit and a linen shirt monogrammed with his initials, he would truly be a testament to sophistication and good taste.

The banker probably spent time before dinner engaged in financial conversations, this being his favorite subject. He would lend advice to someone and possibly pick up a stock market tip from fellow guests.

The seasoned sleuth always tries to reconstruct a crime scene, but with this one, there is little to go on. All reports, books, and stories say the same thing. After dinner on the evening of July 30, Piper purchased a cigar from a stand in the hotel lobby, stepped outside onto the hotel porch, and was never seen again.

We were not able to determine exactly when Piper was missed, but surely by the next morning after breakfast was served, the stagecoach packed, and the visitors assembled, his absence was noticed. We know a call was made to park authorities and the cavalry was dispatched to search for him. The search continued for a month, but by September no trace of him had been found and the search was abandoned. Interviews with the hotel staff and other guests no doubt were conducted and the conclusion was obviously the same. He just vanished!

During the park's investigation, Mrs. Piper wired Mr. J. H. Dean, the Yellowstone Park Association manager, and offered a reward of $1,000 for the return of her husband or the remains of his body. As a last attempt to find her husband, Mrs. Piper sent her brother to the park to conduct his own investigation. Piper's brother-in-law traveled to Yellowstone and questioned everyone he could, following every possible lead. For nearly a month he even slept outdoors, hoping he could somehow follow the howls of coyotes and find the remains of his brother-in-law. He found nothing. In December Piper was given up for dead.

What really happened to Piper? Did he meet someone who later followed him into the darkness and murdered him for his expensive jewelry and cash? Was his body dumped into a nearby hot pool to get rid of it? Perhaps after his own dinner he became dinner for the grizzly bear that frequented the garbage dump in back of the hotel. Perhaps Piper accidentally came across the grizzly bear in the dark, and the startled bear killed Piper and dragged away his body to feast on later. Or maybe Piper just stepped into the black night and, not knowing the area very well, fell into one of the hot pools all by himself, his body disintegrating in the boiling water.

Not knowing what happened to LeRoy R. Piper is disturbing enough, but knowing there will never be an ending to his story is somewhat bizarre. That's what makes his story a true Yellowstone mystery. Perhaps Piper's ghost is in the steam that floats across the Lower Geyser Basin, forever trying to find its way back to the comfort and safety of the Fountain Hotel.

MATTIE'S SPIRIT

There are eight individual graves known to be scattered throughout Yellowstone National Park. One in particular has been shrouded in mystery and myth. This lonely grave is found on the banks of the Firehole River near the Nez Perce Picnic Area off Fountain Flat Drive. Every year, thousands of tourists discover the grave, which, along with other statistical information, bares the name of Mattie. Some have seen it while picnicking. Others have sought it out after hearing or reading stories about her. But whatever brought them to her, most have said they have not been the same since visiting her grave. Mattie's spirit seems to draw one back. Who is Mattie? Where did she come from? Why is she buried alone?

Mattie was born Martha Jane Shipley on September 18, 1856, but the name Mattie agreed with her more, and she was known as Mattie all of her life. When her life ended, "Mattie" was lovingly used to mark her place of rest.

Mattie's life was not easy. She was born to British immigrants in Massachusetts. Her family worked in dirty textile mills where the air was filled with the deadly germs of tuberculosis, commonly called white lung. The Shipleys often moved in search of better wages and better working conditions. While she was still very young, Mattie's parents separated, and Mattie lived with her father until the Civil War began. When she was seven, Mattie's father was killed in the war, forcing her and her siblings to live with other families.

Mattie learned the textile trade. Years later, she and her older sister Millie decided it was time for a change. Millie had met a young man named David Alston, and the three decided to begin a new life out west. Mattie had no idea of the future that awaited her in beautiful Montana, but she knew it would be a healthy change from the textile mills. Perhaps she already suspected that she was infected with tuberculosis. She had heard that moving to a dryer climate would bring some comfort and maybe even a cure.

Mattie helped her sister and brother-in-law homestead in Pease Bottom, Montana, near Billings. This was where Mattie met and married Eugene Gillett in 1882, and then tragically lost him a year later to tuberculosis. It wasn't an easy time for Mattie. Months turned into a year as she, alone, was left to settle her husband's estate and put her own affairs in order. Mattie was living in the Park Hotel in Billings when she started keeping company with the recently appointed hotel manager, Ellery Culver. Culver had many of the same experiences as a child, losing his parents and growing up in other people's families. Ellery, a widower, no doubt took quick notice of the spirited 26-year-old Mattie.

As Mattie and Ellery spent more time together, she learned that Ellery had served in the Civil War like her father and had worked for the Northern Pacific Railroad as had her first husband Eugene. What a coincidence that their lives so paralleled! They were two souls who had been left behind by their loved ones, but it seemed to give them common ground to build a relationship. They were married on April 6, 1886.

After the wedding, Mattie and Ellery moved into their own house on the south side of town and Mattie joined her husband in civic duties, ranching, and even some hunting and fishing. By winter, the Culvers were preparing for their first child. On June 22, 1887, they welcomed with love little Theda Culver. Soon after the birth of their daughter, Ellery packed up and left for Yellowstone National Park. He had accepted the position of Master of Transportation with the Yellowstone Park Association. On July 26, with little Theda in arms, Mattie boarded the train for Livingston and eventually Cinnabar. From there she took a stagecoach eight miles to Mammoth Hot Springs and finally to the Firehole Basin where she was reunited with her beloved Ellery.

This was most likely Mattie's first visit to Yellowstone, and it must have been one of the most exciting times of her life. Aside from the discomfort of the dust from riding on the stagecoach, it was no doubt indescribable to witness the park in its pristine beauty. The Culver family took up seasonal residence in a hotel that practically sat on the banks of the Firehole River. It was the second hotel in the area built by George Marshall. Originally called Marshall's Place, it had changed hands a few times and was now owned by the Yellowstone Park Association. The Association called it the Firehole Hotel, and it was a perfect place to spend the summer. Here Mattie and Ellery could see nature at its best. With wildlife so abundant and the geysers playing day and night, they had truly found a haven.

As autumn drew near, Mattie, Ellery, and little Theda returned to Billings. They rented a house and easily slipped back into the routine of city life. By April 1888, Mattie and Ellery were celebrating their second wedding anniversary and busily preparing for their return to Yellowstone. And by this time, Mattie must have known she was dying.

Mattie knew the symptoms. She knew she had tuberculosis. She could have caught it anywhere, for at the time most people knew very little of how contagious tuberculosis was. She could have carried it from her textile days or contracted it from her first husband, Eugene. But that was not important now. She needed to prepare herself and her family for her death. Treatments for tuberculosis were many, but cures were none.

Ellery's job caused him to travel to Livingston and Billings, but Mattie may have been too ill to accompany him on those trips so she and Theda stayed in the park. As the chilling fall winds began to blow, it was decided that Mattie, Ellery, and little Theda would spend the winter at the hotel as winter-keepers.

We do not know how sick Mattie became before her death, or what it must have been like for Ellery as he watched his beautiful companion's life slip away. Mattie died on March 2, 1889, and although her tombstone indicates she was thirty years old, she was in fact thirty-two. The pain of both Ellery and their little daughter Theda cannot be imagined. Mattie died a little shy of her third wedding anniversary.

Soldiers at the nearby station came over and did what they could, but the snow was deep and the ground much too frozen to dig a grave. Finding two large barrels, they laid them end to end, put Mattie's body inside, and covered them with snow. About a week later a friend and co-worker, R. R. Cummins, helped Ellery prepare a proper grave as best as they could. Her coffin was made from a partition in the hotel she lived in, loved in, and cared for. A brief service was given and she was tenderly laid to rest near the riverbank about a stone's throw from the old Firehole Hotel. Ellery stayed at the hotel with their year-old daughter until April. Then they went west so Theda could live with Mattie's sister, Millie, and her family, who had moved to Washington State. Later, Mrs. H. W. Child, wife of an early park concessionaire, had a fence build around Matte's grave.

Ellery stayed with Theda at her Aunt Millie's but soon felt Mattie's spirit and heard her beckoning call. He returned to her and continued working in and around the park, always heeding Mattie's haunting call.

In 1891, being obsolete, the old Firehole Hotel was burned down, giving way for the new Fountain Hotel a few miles up the road. This change left Mattie's grave in solitude.

Ellery visited Theda often but always returned to Mattie and the Yellowstone they both loved so much. Tragedy again visited Ellery in 1906 when at only nineteen, Theda became ill. Hearing her mother's call, Theda followed her mother in death.

Ellery worked three more years near Mattie in Yellowstone. Finally, age and health dictated that he move to the old soldiers home in California. He lived there only a short time and on April 17, 1922, Ellery answered his dearest Mattie's call for the last time and returned to her arms forever.

Ellery could not be buried next to Mattie. The National Park Service forbade it. He was buried in the National Soldier's Home Cemetery in what is now Los Angeles. But those who have visited his grave know he is not there. The love Mattie and Ellery had for each other endured 33 years while they were worlds apart. Now, after being united in death, Ellery and Mattie are together in the place they loved.

Many who have visited Yellowstone are repeatedly drawn to Mattie's grave. Her spirit, now joined by Ellery's, can sometimes be seen walking along the riverbank. Some say they've heard Mattie humming lullabies to baby birds in the trees. It's impossible to visit Mattie's grave and not feel her strong spirit beckoning you to return. Some do return and bring flowers, others quietly meditate, but all eventually return.

THE HAUNTING OF OLD FAITHFUL INN

Among the vast species of the un-dead, ghosts are the most popular forms, and places with history naturally become "ghost collectors." Through the years, the Old Faithful Inn has collected its share of shadows. It surely seems fitting that such a hospitable old place would become a sanctuary for tired souls and un-resting spirits. To date, there have been at least three spirits encountered in the inn. The interesting thing about these spirits is that they all seem to dwell in different time dimensions and are unaware of one another. Here are their stories.

THE PHANTOM CHILD

The youngest and newest spirit to take up residence is that of a boy. The young specter's story was revealed late one evening while researching information on another spirit. While walking in the Old Faithful Inn, I met a young auburn-haired lady from Georgia. She told me about the phantom child. She confessed that because she had worked the graveyard shift most of the summer, she had not seen this little phantom. But she assured me that many of her friends had, and they had told her about him.

Every summer, thousands of families visit Yellowstone National Park. No vacation is complete without the traditional stop at Upper Geyser Basin to spend a few hours walking around the thermal area and watching Old Faithful, the world's most famous geyser. After the eruption, a brisk walk through the comfy old inn is a must. It's fun to sit and relax while the inn's huge clock ticks away or take in the awesome view of the geyser basin from the second floor observation porch. But while on the second floor, keep an eye out for the little lost phantom child.

This strange little ghost is peculiar in the fact that unlike a typical apparition (if there is really such a thing as a typical apparition), he appears only in the day. He is about three or four years old and stands three feet tall. He is wearing shorts, a tee shirt and Keds sneakers. You won't see him coming but you will suddenly feel his presence. You turn around and there he is.

He is lost, he tells you, and he can't find his mommy or daddy. You ask him his parents' names...but he will tell you nothing. So you ask him his name...and still there is silence. Then you decide it's time to get help. You assure the little boy that everything will be all right as big tears start to slide down his face. You take his little hand and start for the information desk. When you arrive, you explain to the clerk that this little boy has lost his parents, and as you both look for the child holding your hand...he has disappeared into thin air. Feeling embarrassed, you try to explain. But an explanation is not necessary, because this is not new.

Our phantom has been trying to find his family for more than thirty years. He has appeared to hotel guests as well as those visitors who have just stepped in for ice cream.

Of all who have seen the boy, three things are constant. He seems to have an accent, he haunts only the second floor mezzanine, and he only appears once to them. In fact, many have gone back to search for him, but he is nowhere to be found.

THE HEADLESS BRIDE

The headless bride of Old Faithful Inn is one of my favorite stories. It's about a mysterious but timid young lady. We first read of her in a local newspaper more than ten years ago. Fascinated, we started asking questions. Most of the staff at the inn knew some of her story, but no one knew much. We finally traced it to George.

George is the author of this sad tale of the lonely apparition. At the time we spoke to him, he was the inn's manager. He told us that the Headless Bride appeared at the insistence of visitors who for years pressed him for a ghost story. Little did he know that his beautiful and haunting spirit would endure for decades.

During the fall of 1982, George was a bellman and he was finishing up the summer season. He and another employee were closing the inn in preparation for the long winter ahead. While reading in his room a little past midnight, George heard someone down the hall.

Knowing that everyone was supposed to be gone, he put down his book and walked to the balcony overlooking the lobby. Looking in all directions, he saw nothing so he returned to his room and his book. Fifteen minutes later, he heard the same noise. Once again he put down the book, went out to the balcony, and this time checked the halls of the old house. Again he saw nothing. Finally, returning to his room, he heard the noise again and it was louder than ever.

George ran onto the balcony, where he was just in time to see a transparent figure ascend from the crow's nest high above the lobby. The figure was draped in a white flowing gown. It was a young woman, not much older than a child. And she was carrying, tucked under her arm...her head!

George called out for the other employee, and they left the inn that minute and did not return. That winter, while doing research in the library at Missoula, Montana, George discovered there had been a death, perhaps even a murder, at the inn in the summer of 1914. It took place in room 127. A couple who had just gotten married came there to spend their honeymoon. What seemed to be a grand and glorious day for the two newlyweds eventually turned into a nightmare. There was an argument, a fight, and the groom left, never to return.

It was thought by everyone that his young bride, overcome with grief, had locked herself in their room, refusing food or service of any kind. After a few days, the staff became rather worried about the young lady, so the manager sent a member of the housekeeping staff to room 127 to see if she could be of assistance. When the young bride would not answer the door, the housekeeper opened it...and found the young bride lying in the bathtub in a pool of blood...without her head.

In time, more pieces of the tale surfaced. Investigations found that the young girl of 15 was the only child of a rich and affluent family, and she was heir to a million-dollar shipping firm in New York City. She had fallen in love, however, with a family servant much older than she. Their affair was discovered and the girl immediately fell from her father's grace. He saw through the ambitious man's plans of marriage in order to join the family business.

The daughter refused to listen to her father and insisted they be wed. So the father agreed to a quiet wedding and sent them west for a honeymoon and life without further family embarrassment. By the time the couple had reached Yellowstone and the inn, the young man had managed to gamble away all of the money which was meant to last them until he could obtain employment and procure property.

The young bride was sent by her husband to contact her father by telegram and petition for more money. Her father refused to send money but instead offered to send a train ticket for his daughter to return home. At this news the husband became livid and the couple fought all night. When the sun rose the next morning, the young bride was dead and her groom had disappeared.

The bride's father was notified by park officials, and he arrived, heartbroken, a few days later. All news concerning his daughter's death was hushed to discourage any chance of scandal.

Eventually the bride's missing head was found in a corner of the Crow's Nest at the inn, but by then her body had already been disposed. When all of his daughter's affairs had been put in order, the father returned to the family home in New York City. His life resumed as though nothing had happened, and his daughter was not spoken of again.

Now, almost a century later, it is late in the Old Faithful Inn as the pianist puts away his music and the lobby and mezzanines slowly become deserted. There are far off echoes of dishes from the closed dining room, and the night clerk at the front desk looks over tomorrow's checkouts. Someone from housekeeping straightens the chairs around the gigantic fireplace.

Everything is in order, just like every other night. And, just like every other night, promptly at midnight, she appears. But only those who believe in her see her as she slowly ascends the Crow's Nest. She seems to be floating, but one cannot be sure. What is sure is that she is headless. As she reaches the bottom step she turns, and then you can see what she has tucked under her arm...her head.

They say she haunts only the "Old House," which is the original part of the inn. This, of course, is because it existed at the time of her death. She seems to roam endlessly, looking for her husband. Finally, standing just outside her room, she realizes he has not returned, and she sadly disappears.

THE HUSBAND RETURNS

Perhaps the story isn't over. You see, the third ghost at the Old Faithful Inn may be connected to our bride. While tracking down her story in 1994, I went on a tour through the inn. After the tour, I asked the guide what she knew about the bride or any other haunting. I was quickly assured there were none. Knowing different, I went to the information desk and inquired there. I was surprised when the young redheaded employee said, "You mean the sailor?"

Well, that was a whole different story and I asked him what he knew. He said in the 1970s reports started coming from the staff and visitors that someone or something was frequenting the halls of the inn, rattling doors and shaking windows. At first it was thought it was the inn's security staff checking to make sure everything was tightly closed up.

Then the first sighting occurred. It was of an older gentleman, a sailor type, dressed in merchant marine clothing of the early 20th century. Most encounters were by those who spotted him inside the inn, checking unlocked rooms. But others found him outside, peering through the windows. The bizarre thing is that this man, when described, was a much older version of our 1914 groom who beheaded his bride and fled into the night. Could this be the same ambitious man, the man who selfishly took his young bride from her parents...who stole her youth...and then ended her life? If so, then after more than eighty years his soul has returned as an old, tormented spirit doomed to be exiled in the very place where he committed his horrible crime.

Perhaps it is the husband's punishment to search through the Old Faithful Inn for his bride, perhaps to somehow make amends. If so, he searches in vain. For their deaths took place in different decades, and their spirits will never meet because they each haunt different dimensions, and dimensions seldom intersect.

DEAD MEN DON'T PLAY POKER

Legends are stories or tales from earlier times. They are preserved by tradition and are thought to be somewhat historical. In his second volume of *The Yellowstone Story*, Aubrey Haines related an incident that he labeled "an enduring Yellowstone Legend."

There are very few who spend any length of time studying Yellowstone National Park who don't run across Mr. Haines' name and learn quickly that he is probably the foremost authority on the history of the park. So, when he says this is a legend, that's good enough for this author. However, considering that the story has endured almost 100 years is further testament to its authenticity as one of Yellowstone's true legends.

In April 1904, Private Richard R. Hurley, a soldier at the Snake River station, became ill with dysentery. Now this story, as with other legends, has two different versions.

The first version says that the soldier's illness continued to worsen until the sergeant in charge, realizing that Hurley needed a doctor's care, dispatched a team of soldiers to transport Hurley to Fort Yellowstone at Mammoth. On the way, Hurley died at the West Thumb emergency cabin.

The second version tells us that although Hurley was sick, no one thought that he was seriously ill. So having to go out on a routine patrol, the soldiers left Hurley with food and wood. Upon returning, they found Hurley frozen to death in the station. He had been trying to make a fire.

For the record, archives of Fort Yellowstone list Hurley as dying May 3, 1904, at the emergency cabin at West Thumb.

In any case, the soldiers now had the frozen body of Private Hurley of the F Company, Third Division, and the chore of transporting that body to Fort Yellowstone for burial. The soldiers set out heading north, dragging old Hurley behind them, but once again we come to two versions. One story is that they ended up at the Norris station, while another story puts them at Fountain. Either way, neither story disputes the fact that after a long day in the cold, the soldiers were ready for a shot or two of whiskey and a good old poker game.

As the evening wore on and their spirits lightened up a bit, someone suggested that old Joe (the dead soldier) might want to join the game. So his frozen body was propped up and leaned against the window, and during every round a hand of poker was dealt to the dead man.

The story goes that the soldiers played poker until ten o'clock the next morning, when old dead Joe, who was still leaning against the window, received the warming benefit of the morning sun and started to thaw. Slowly Joe's hand moved as if laying down his cards, and the frightened soldiers ran for the door!

THE GREAT ABSAROKA
DEFIANCE

Although there is no real historical documentation of the following story, some say it is a legend shared among the Absaroka tribes for many years. It is written as it might have been told by an old Chief to his children:

In a time long ago, our people camped and hunted in the land of the Great Yellowstone. They revered the spouting waters and hissing steam. The giant mountains were havens for our ancestors' spirits, for from the peaks one could see far into the next world. Surrounded by these mountains, our people felt safe and secure, for it was here that their own grandfathers had camped and hunted. It was here where their grandmothers raised strong sons and daughters. It was here along the Yellowstone River they were one with their generous Mother Earth. The Absaroka did not believe the earth belonged to them, but rather, they belonged to her. The mountains and the meadows were sacred with holy reflections of those ancestors who went before. They shared the earth with every living creature. To our people all creatures are our brothers and we are equal to all living things on Mother Earth.

As the white man came westward, they found Yellowstone. The government in Washington soon felt struggles with our people. So the Army leaders sent men to sit in council with the leaders of the Absaroka and a treaty was written on white man's paper. On this paper, boundaries were set for the Crow Indian Nation, and land along the Yellowstone River was given to us. The land stretched as far as the tops of the great Absaroka Mountains. It was not long before the white man's treaty was forgotten and soon more white men came. This caused more fighting, so the Army sent troops. They pushed and crowded our once mighty and proud people to flat, barren lands with poor fishing and few buffalo. As our people were corralled by the soldiers, a band of warriors escaped and took refuge along the upper Yellowstone.

Learning of this, the soldiers chased them. The government wanted to keep all of our people on the reservation according to the white man's treaty. They felt that the warrior braves should be punished for escaping the reservation. After many days of being chased, and many nights without sleep, there were only a few warriors still alive. One evening in council, it was decided they should run no more. The brave warriors gathered at the head of the Grand Canyon of the Great Yellowstone River, and there each warrior, young and old, agreed to take his own life rather than surrender to the white man and live caged on the reservation.

Days passed and together they built a fine raft from the trunks of the lodgepole pines growing along the

Yellowstone. When it was finished, they carried it to the brink of the Lower Falls. There they shared many favorite stories of wisdom from their Fathers and Grandfathers before them. But those days were not to last. From a distance, they could hear the thunder of horses and knew the white soldiers were coming. It was now time to be carried to their deaths as they had planned. When the sun awakened them the next morning, each warrior took his place on the raft and pushed off into the rushing waters. Prepared to meet the Great Father and their ancestors, they rode the swift current that took them to the next world. Those with guns shot them off in defiance against all in captivity while the white soldiers standing on the riverbank looked in bewilderment. The warriors had chosen the ultimate escape, and turning to their enemy, with great defiance, they chanted their last song and stood tall as the rush of the rapids sent them surging 308 feet to the rocks below.

As seasons pass, the legend remains. Each time you stand in wonder of the great Lower Falls of the Yellowstone, feel the power and strength of our warriors...hear their echoing chants of freedom and prayers for peace...look for the faces of the brave warrior spirits who stood together in defiance of injustice, and who chose eternal freedom that morning in Yellowstone.

THE VANISHING HITCHHIKER

Ghosts are known to return from beyond the grave to render help or deliver important messages. Stories describe these specters as protective spirits who watch over families and guide travelers. The familiar Vanishing Hitchhiker story tells of a mysterious young lady in distress. The legend originated around the turn of the century somewhere east of the Mississippi River and seems to resurrect each decade, updated to fit the era. In the 1930s, for example, the horse-drawn carriage was changed to the automobile. Each time as the story emerges and spreads throughout the country it is modified to include familiar surroundings and local landmarks. Here is our version.

On July 22, 1994, Marc Elliot was in the Albright Visitors Center at Mammoth Hot Springs when he heard a loud clap of thunder. He looked out the window just in time to see a cloudburst drench the sidewalk. Glancing at the clock, he realized it was late. "Better head for the Lake Hotel now," he thought. "Maybe I can still get there before dark."

Marc dashed through the rain and jumped into his classic scarlet Mustang. He only had one more day in the park before he had to leave for home. He flipped on his headlights and settled back. He knew he had quite a drive and he hoped the rain would lighten up.

Marc couldn't believe it was so dark. It was only four o'clock in the afternoon. He remembered a conversation with a park ranger at Old Faithful. The ranger said they could have the most horrid rainstorms in Yellowstone and then an hour later it would clear up and be beautiful. He looked forward to that but right now the rain was so thick he could hardly see in front of the car. He turned on his bright headlights and turned up his windshield wipers. The rain was fierce.

Suddenly, out of nowhere, something was in front of his car. At first it appeared almost formless, and then Marc realized it was a person...yes, a woman standing in the road! Marc slammed on his brakes but it was too late. He must have hit her because she appeared so close, so suddenly. Marc closed his eyes, thinking, "Oh no! I've killed her!"

Marc stopped the car and got out. The woman was gone. Was it a dream? No! He saw her and there was no way he could have avoided hitting her.

Marc kneeled down to inspect his car. There was no body underneath it. No dent in the front. No blood. As he got up he practically stepped into a woman...the one that was nowhere in sight seconds ago! He felt a chill, perhaps from the rain, perhaps from the scare of the accident.

With a far-off glance and a hollow smile, the woman asked for a ride. Still trying to compose himself, Marc assured her it was no place for man or beast and agreed to give her a lift. Noticing the young lady was soaked, Marc opened the car door and grabbed his raincoat. He wrapped it around her and helped her into the car. Marc got in and started carefully down the road. The rain was not letting up. He traveled at a snail's pace while she sat beside him and stared out the window.

Marc asked where she was headed. She told him she was on her way to the Canyon Hotel where she was a waitress. Marc glanced at her long full skirt. He thought how clever it was for the hotel staff to wear clothes that were of the 1900s. He broke the silence by asking her name and how she came to be stranded so far from the hotel.

She said her name was Victoria Venable and that she was an employee of the Yellowstone Park Hotel Company. She was from the Mammoth area and had been waiting for her ride to pick her up. When she realized that she'd been forgotten, she decided to start walking in hope that someone would notice her and give her a ride. Marc admitted that he had definitely noticed her but suggested that the next time she stand on the side of the rode and not in the middle. The young lady smiled weakly, coughed, and stared out the window. Marc was worried about her cough. He suggested she see a doctor. She thanked him for his concern but said the cough was an old one.

The rain turned to snow. At the summit of the road, the woman screamed, "Stop!" Marc slammed on the brakes just in time to miss three bighorn sheep that leaped across the road. He knew that if she hadn't warned him, he would have plowed into the animals or, worse, the car could have gone off the road and killed them both. Swallowing his heart, he turned to Victoria and thanked her. She smiled. At Canyon Junction, Victoria directed Marc to the hotel. Music and laughter could be heard from inside. He asked if he could see her again. Victoria smiled and kissed him, then stepped out of the car, walked into the hotel, and disappeared into the crowd.

As Marc drove away he couldn't forget Victoria's sudden warning and the impossibly safe stop he made. How could she have known? No one could have seen those sheep in the blinding rain. She had saved their lives and he was grateful. But more than that, he was intrigued. There was something about her. He had to see her again.

By the time Marc reached Lake Hotel, he was both physically and emotionally drained. It had been an exhausting day. Entering the hotel, he noticed the beautiful period-style furniture, but the staff wore modern attire. Why didn't this staff wear turn-of-the-century clothing like the staff at Canyon Hotel? He questioned the desk clerk, but she had no idea what he was talking about.

A bellman took the luggage. Marc followed him to the elevator and asked how they had weathered the storm. The bellman said it had been sunny all day. Entering his room, Marc looked out the window. Not a drop of water had fallen. Everything was dry. Marc was confused. He tried to sleep but visions of Victoria kept creeping into his thoughts.

The next morning, Marc felt good. He was going to find Victoria. His excuse to see her was his raincoat. She still had it. At the front desk Marc explained the situation and asked the clerk to check and see if there were any rooms available for that night at Canyon Hotel. The clerk look puzzled. Another clerk overheard the conversation and explained there was no Canyon Hotel. It had burned down years ago.

Marc bolted out the door, jumped in his car, and headed north to the hotel. He drove as fast as he could but the traffic was slow and it seemed like hours before he reached the area. He wasn't sure exactly where the hotel stood, but he knew if he came to the Canyon Junction he had gone too far. Suddenly, there was the road to the hotel. He followed it up the slight hill, but at the end of the parking lot there was no hotel, just a few horses in a corral flanked by two very small buildings.

Marc couldn't believe it. He got out of the car and ran to where the hotel had stood the night before. Where was it? How could it have disappeared?

Searching for answers, Marc walked through the grass and found only broken blocks of cement belonging to the hotel's once grand, mile-round foundation.

Hurt and confused, Marc drove to Mammoth and found the Yellowstone Library. He asked for information about the hotel and was given a book and a few old magazines. They confirmed what he had been told. The hotel had been sold for a mere $25 in 1959 and then it had mysteriously burned to the ground in 1960.

The lump in his throat turned into a pound in his heart. If the hotel wasn't real, was the girl? And if she wasn't real, where was his coat?

Marc left the library and walked across the street to a picnic table. He sat down to think. Gradually he realized he was sitting near a young woman and that she had an uncanny resemblance to Victoria. He stared at her. She was reading a book but kept glancing at him. Finally she asked if anything was wrong. Marc apologized for his rudeness. He told her the events of the past twenty-four hours and said she looked very much like Victoria.

She smiled strangely and said, "Really? I was just reading about an employee whose name was Victoria who worked at the Canyon Hotel a long time ago."

Marc looked at the book. It was *Death in Yellowstone*. The woman showed Marc the page where Victoria was listed as being buried in the Fort Yellowstone Army Cemetery. She had been a waitress at the Canyon Hotel and she had died on July 22, 1914—eighty years ago to the day that Marc met her.

Obtaining directions from the young lady, Marc drove to the old cemetery. It was a small, gated enclosure on a lazily sloping hill. As he got out of his car and approached, he noticed something draped over one of the headstones. It was his raincoat.

Marc walked to the grave, picked up his raincoat, and read the name inscribed on the headstone: "Victoria Venable." Immediately he heard a clap of thunder. Yes, he thought, it was almost time for her to go to work. He told Victoria goodbye, wished her peace...and left.

THE PIRATE OF YELLOWSTONE LAKE

Certain spirits are doomed to remain on earth eternally, some because they refuse to accept the fact that they are dead and others because they will not give up something important and of value to them. The story of Ella C. Waters' cursed and loathsome old soul is a story of the latter. There is a considerable amount of material on E. C. Waters in the Yellowstone National Park library which documents his dishonest dealings and exposes him as a disgusting, stingy old coot who, because of his selfishness, may never leave his earthly haunting.

Whatever slimy rock Waters crawled out from under is not known for sure, but folks believed him to be from Wisconsin. There is also talk that he was booted out of the Union Army shortly after the Civil War ended. Somehow though, he ended up twenty-two years later in Montana. Most everyone who knew him called him a no good pirate. Some hated him, some feared him, and most considered him insane.

We don't know exactly when Waters became associated with the park. Records show him causing trouble as early as 1886. He liked bullying people. He was a man of very little moral character, bouncing from one job to another. No one wanted him because no one trusted him. But he was like a bad penny, always around and impossible to get rid of.

For a while Waters served as the manager of the Mammoth Hotel, but the complaints about him were downright scandalous. Patrons and employees talked of how he would often leave at sundown with some poor girl from his staff and then end up spending the night with her somewhere. Finally Waters was fired after a member of the park association called his mismanagement a "disgrace to the Association."

Even so, another time Waters served briefly as the association's general manager but was quickly removed by Captain Boutelle, the park superintendent, for reasons which included the mismanagement of the construction of the Lake Hotel. Sadly enough, his dismissal was short lived as Captain Boutelle was soon transferred to another post.

With Boutelle gone, Waters was again free to seize opportunities. This time he managed to confiscate the position of president of the Yellowstone Boat Company. In addition, he obtained a lease for the land he needed and somehow seemed to operate free from the reins of the Yellowstone Park Association. It seems that what Waters couldn't swindle through lies and deceit, he commandeered with intimidation and harassment. The man was now in a prime position. Although he did not actually own the Yellowstone Lake Boat Company, he was in control. His company did very well at first, for many visitors looked forward to boat trips on Yellowstone Lake between West Thumb and Lake Hotel, a quicker and more comfortable alternative to the dusty old coaches called tallyhos.

It seemed that renting rowboats and running a steamboat on the lake would be a lucrative business, and so it was. By 1897 the Yellowstone Boat Company somehow ended up belonging to Waters. He had a fleet of rowboats and a passenger boat named the *Zillah*. His business and boats were always in disrepair, but he managed enough capital to keep comfortable himself and his family, which lived in Wisconsin most of the time. He also continued to snare more concession leases.

At the turn of the century, however, when most park concessions were somewhat stable, E. C. Waters' Yellowstone Lake Boat Company showed definite signs of sinking. Waters became even more demanding and impossible to deal with. In desperation, he raised his already excessive prices. He offered the tallyho drivers fifty cents a head for every tourist they could lure aboard his *Zillah*. He brazenly charged each passenger one fare to board his boat and another fare to disembark at the other shore. Attempting to keep even more money, he stopped paying the commissions to the tallyho drivers and they ended up boycotting him.

Old Waters' next attempt to turn a buck was to throw together a makeshift zoo consisting of some buffalo and elk that he placed on Dot Island in Yellowstone Lake. Waters docked at the island en route to the Lake Hotel and charged his passengers admission. However, protests were lodged about the filthy and inhumane way in which the animals were treated. Tourists complained about having to watch starving animals literally fight for potato peelings and other scraps that Waters provided. Finally, after being served with a government order, Waters was forced to release the animals.

By this time Waters was desperate. He stirred up rumors about the railroad monopolizing the park. He cried that the proposed road from West Thumb to Lake was a deliberate act to run him out of business. The never-ending complaints from angry customers were tearing down his business. Many visitors branded him a rogue and a fraud and refused to risk a ride in his old, run-down boat. When news of these circumstances finally reached Washington, it was suggested that Waters was indeed a nuisance and most likely had a mental disorder.

In 1905 another problem plagued Waters. Word came west that his 18-year-old daughter Anna had taken her own life at the family home in Wisconsin by taking chloroform followed by a dose of carbolic acid. Waters was quick to blame the suicide on the stress caused by the family's pending financial ruin and the many humiliating accusations about him. It's interesting to note that Waters also had a son who took his own life, but we know nothing of where or when that happened.

After his daughter's death, Waters suddenly came up with money to buy a new steamboat, which he conceitedly named after himself, the *E. C. Waters*. It was delivered to the Yellowstone Lake Boat Company and Waters boasted that the new steamer could easily accommodate many more people and this was going to finally make him the wealthy man he knew he deserved to be.

When park officials only licensed the *E. C. Waters* to carry 125 people, just a few more than the number he already crammed into the *Zillah*, Waters was infuriated! He refused to operate the steamer and permanently docked it on the east side of Stevenson Island. In his anger, to insure it would never be used by anyone, Waters hacked the boat full of holes.

Waters, now a dejected man, ran the Yellowstone Lake Boat Company only two more years. By then he had managed to estrange many of the other concessionaires, park employees, and even his own crew. The beginning of the end had come, and when he offended a congressman from New York, he fell out of grace with Washington for the last time.

In 1907 President Roosevelt expelled him from the park, and he was forbidden to return without written permission from the Secretary of the Interior. Waters' boat concession was canceled and given to T. E. Hofer, who bought him out the following year. Waters spent three years in court trying to get back what he felt had been wrongfully taken, but he was unsuccessful. Historical notes point to his returning to his home in Wisconsin.

While researching this story a few summers ago, we toured Yellowstone Lake via the scenic cruise out of

Bridge Bay. During the tour, we circled Stevenson Island and the guide pointed out the old rusted *E. C. Waters* still lying half sunk in a sandy grave. How sad, to be built for many, but in actuality, to carry no one. We learned that twenty years after the boat was abandoned the boilers were removed and used in the heating system of the Lake Hotel. The old steamer, rusted and weathered, was eventually burned.

After the tour, I shared with our guide the purpose of our visit. He confided that he'd met a grandson of one of Waters' crew who said that his grandfather said old Waters died in an insane asylum in Milwaukee, Wisconsin. This may be true, but the old pirate's spirit has returned to the island. He just couldn't give it up and is still guarding what's left of that old skeleton of a boat. Some have said that if you stand on the shoreline of Yellowstone Lake at dusk and the wind is blowing just right, you can hear old Waters bemoaning his ill fate. Later, towards midnight, you can see a tiny glow of a kindled fire on Stevenson Island where the Yellowstone pirate tries unsuccessfully to warm his ghostly soul.

A GRAVE STORY

There is a short trail leading east from the majestic Lake Hotel past an old gas station to a quaint little Hamilton store. It is used by guests and employees because it is a fast route to a quick snack or souvenir. Along this trail is a lonely grave. It's just a mound of dirt and rocks with a wooden cross. No one seems to know exactly when it appeared or where it came from. The strange thing is...no one is buried there. The body that should be buried there has been lost.

Actually, lost isn't quite accurate. The body is buried somewhere east of the hotel. All evidence puts it under the present parking area of the gas station. It may even be under the gas station itself. Authorities simply don't know.

The body is of a man named Dave Edwards. Very little is known about him, and his life seems almost as mysterious as his death. There is no record that Edwards had a wife or family. All we know is that he lived alone in a cabin on Stevenson Island in Yellowstone Lake. Remnants of his cabin on the island can still be found. He lived in solitude, making Edwards a man of true mystery.

Edwards was employed by E. C. Waters of the Yellowstone Lake Boat Company. He had a variety of responsibilities, including winter-keeper of the Yellowstone Boat Company's facilities. Because of his employer's crass and vulgar manner, Edwards' job must have been difficult and far from satisfying. It would be tough to work for such terrible man.

Every day Edwards rowed his small boat from his cabin on Stevenson Island to the docks. He did his job and rowed back to his cabin without making much of an impression on anyone. But it's the eerie events which have occurred since his death that have been making a great impression on Yellowstone and those who visit and work there. National Park Service records show on November 12, 1906, Edwards died in his rowboat while rowing to Stevenson Island. He apparently suffered a heart attack. Soldiers who were working at Lake Station saw his drifting rowboat, investigated, and found Edwards' body in the boat.

Being so late in the tourist season, it was lucky that Edwards' body was found at all. At this point in our story the facts become less clear. Evidently Edwards was buried at Lake because it was noted that his employer, Waters, was intent on "exhuming" the body in the spring to send it Edwards' hometown, believed to be Alta, Iowa. But there is no evidence that Waters ever did so.

About a year after Edwards's death, the Yellowstone Lake Boat Company was sold and Waters was kicked out of the park. The body of Dave Edwards remained buried near the lake.

Years passed, and old Dave Edwards still lay peacefully in his grave. Then, as more development took place in the area, a crew was sent to upgrade the roads, including building an access road to a new store. The work required paving over the area where Edwards' grave was located, and plans called for the grave to be relocated. But it wasn't, at least not completely.

Instead, park concessionaire Charles Hamilton, who was building the new store, decided to save time and money. He simply picked up the tombstone, moved it a short distance away, placed a picket fence around it and put some memorial flowers on top of it, and left the body in the ground where it was. Edwards' old gravesite was then covered with asphalt.

The separation of the body from the new gravesite left the soul of Dave Edwards without eternal peace. Folklore reminds us that spirits become agitated, restless, and sometimes even vengeful when their final resting place is disturbed. In fact, history is flooded with tales of people, who through desecration of the dead, have often brought ghostly wrath upon themselves and others.

Edwards' ghost appears to have taken no wrath, at least not yet. It's just a lost soul looking for a place to rest...preferably his final place of rest, the place which was taken away from him.

Lately in this area, strange sightings have occurred. When the sun settles in the west and the shadows grow heavy on the lake, the spirit of Dave Edwards appears. He can be seen swinging his dimly lit lantern in the woods, searching for his final resting place. Although his spirit has been felt throughout the Lake area, the ghost has so far only been spotted on the trail east of the hotel. The specter searches from dusk to dawn, sadly looking for its lost grave.

GHOSTLY GUESTS AT LAKE HOTEL

Contrary to most beliefs, few spirits haunt cemeteries, although some are known to visit them often. Another little known ghostly fact is that some souls after death are allowed to choose their place of haunt, while others are inadvertently assigned to theirs. Spirits can be found most anywhere, but they are always there for a purpose.

Topping the list of the more shadowy hangouts are places of birth and places of death, but most haunted places were beloved by the person while they were alive. We've also found that although most ghosts haunt alone, sometimes they can become collective. Collective illusions are souls who join together or unite. They can manifest as one spectral being, a force, or split and take on individual auras of energy. Our opinion is that this story is about a collective of spirits who hold a special love for the beautiful Lake Hotel.

In 1886 a site was chosen for a new hotel on the banks of Yellowstone Lake. Construction on Lake Colonial Hotel began in 1889 and it opened to guests in 1891. At first it was very plain, with little elegance, and resembled other stage-stop hotels in the park. Years later however, renovations and additions transformed it into a grand hotel with just the right touch of southern charm. Today the Lake Hotel is proudly the oldest standing hotel in the park. It is indeed a classical beauty, and it plays host to probably half a dozen mysteriously haunting guests.

In the summer season of 1927, President Calvin Coolidge, his wife, and son visited Yellowstone, and they stayed at the Lake Hotel. It was noted that the President was a very private man. Besides fishing, he was often found in the relaxing solitude of a wonderful wicker rocker, smoking a cigar. The President must have enjoyed himself, because he chose to extend his stay an extra day.

In the 1980s, more than 50 years after President Coolidge's visit, a major restoration project was undertaken and the hotel was restored to its wonderful elegance of the 1920s. Luckily the park still had many of the original pieces of furniture in storage, and they were brought out and used once again. There is a particular old rocker in the lounge that seems to rock by itself. Some think it may be the President.

Some of our spirits are not so famous. In fact, most spectral identities remain an absolute mystery to all. In the early spring of 1990, Anna, a member of the housekeeping staff, was sent along with other employees to prepare rooms for the summer season. After working each day, she always exercised. Because there were only a few employees in the hotel and it was still cold outside, Anna jogged in the halls. One evening as she approached the elevator, she stopped. She said she felt a strong and strange power or energy emitting from what was thought was an empty room. The feeling was so "creepy" it made the hair on her neck stand on end. This frightened her! Anna stared straight ahead, trying not to focus her own energy on the room or its occupant for fear of lending it any more power. Then she quietly spoke to it, saying, "I'm not going to intrude," and she slowly walked down the hall. By the time Anna reached the stairs, she no longer felt the power.

In 1994 a young employee shared his experience of discovering someone watching him from a hotel window. The young man, originally from Eugene, Oregon, was working in the hotel for his second season. By then he thought he had heard all of the local tales about the hotel's ghosts and goblins. Sometimes, he admitted, he even joined in on some practical jokes, even though he didn't believe in ghosts himself. One summer afternoon while outside, he spotted a young child watching him from one of the small windows in the fourth-floor attic. He ran into the hotel and up to the attic but found only a locked door.

A hotel guest once confided that she heard music in the lounge where no one was playing. When she questioned an employee, she was told that the hotel was so old that it was not unusual to be sitting in the lounge alone and hear music of an earlier time. She also confided that she and others even heard dancing music late at night when everyone was settled down for the evening. Years ago, a small instrumental group played each evening in the lounge. Throughout the evening, the group magically transformed into an orchestra as day-shift employees got off work and joined the group with their instruments. Our guess is that these musicians return once in a while to share their talents with those of us who stay at the hotel.

What's more appropriate to haunt than the century-old Yellowstone Lake Hotel? It's the perfect place. Today, we continue to see and hear ghostly visitors. Those spirits, both alone and collective in nature, continuously make it known that they have chosen to visit and perhaps stay. Look for eerie impressions captured in the misty glass carvings throughout the hotel or in the reflections of its imported mirrors. Some souls may be veiled shadows traversing the hallways, while others may be as close as the rocking chair next to you. We may catch them watching us or catch ourselves watching for them. They are the collective spirits who haunt the hotel, spending eternity within its walls.

THE WHISPERS OF YELLOWSTONE LAKE

Within this century, great discoveries have occurred. We can gaze further into space than ever before. Our weather instruments are so accurate they allow us to track weather across the world and forecast storms. In fact, there is really very little that goes on in our atmosphere that scientists cannot see, record, dissect, and explain. But this has not always been the case. Years ago, before we knew as much about our empyrean surroundings, we did not separate spectra and science. Uncertain and even bizarre atmospheric occurrences often were blamed on spirits and the supernatural.

Supernatural or not, the Whispers of Yellowstone Lake have in fact been scientifically documented...but never explained!

The Whispers are described as mystic aerial sounds which rise up from the lake. They come in the early morning when the air is still and the sky is cloudless. The sounds are similar to the vibrations of an electric harp. They are said to start as a low soft hum which can be heard from a great distance. As the hum draws nearer, it becomes louder and louder. Then it passes overhead and slowly starts to die away as it continues in the opposite direction. It lasts no more than a half minute or so.

No one really knows exactly what it is. Many have speculated, trying to label the sound. Some say it's the wind blowing through the trees, but there's no wind. Others have said it sounds like hundreds of swinging telegraph wires, but there are no wires. Some insist it sounds like a swarm of bees, but that's also impossible because the eerie sound often happens in the dead of winter. Others have said it sounds like electricity in the air, or the whistling wings of ducks, or the erupting noise of Steamboat Geyser. Maybe the sound belongs in its own class of aerial echoes.

Since the earliest days of exploration, people have written about the strange lake sounds. Mountain men and fur trappers heard it, and their stories (being somewhat inflated of course) were repeated throughout the country.

Probably one of the first scientific reports of this sound came from a member of the famous Hayden Expedition. Mr. F. H. Bradley, a member of that party, recalled that he heard it one morning during his breakfast. He said it sounded like a "hoarse whine" but he couldn't determine where it was coming from. Later, in 1891, Barton Evermann reported to have heard it.

In 1893 Edwin Linton collected many accounts of the sound and promptly published an article for *Science Magazine*. He heard the sound twice himself and described it as a strange, echoing type of sound in the sky. He also related that it seemed to always die away to the south. Linton asked local mountain guides about it, but they had no idea what it was. Those who had heard it all agreed it was truly one of the most mysterious sounds heard in the mountains.

Although others mentioned the sounds after Linton's report, little was published until Yellowstone photographer Jack Haynes heard the noises himself in 1924. In his *Haynes Guide* he said that he and others were in a boat on Yellowstone Lake near Pelican Roost Island, just off the shore from Steamboat Point in the northeastern part of the lake. It was early in the morning and the lake was mirror still. The sound first rose overhead from the west like a low roar. Becoming louder, it began to rise in pitch. Then it rapidly faded away toward the southwest and, lowering in pitch, it finally silenced. Haynes said it then repeated from another direction and still another sound was heard a third time from another direction. Strangely enough, all this occurred in less than a minute, sounding like nothing he had ever heard before.

In 1935 Ed Henry suggested the eerie sound may be the result of strange air currents caused by the mountain peaks. Henry contacted Hiram Chittenden, who had also studied the sounds, and Chittenden agreed that possibly Henry was right in this theory. Although those who have heard the sounds described them slightly differently, the circumstances and setting have all been similar:

1. They happened when the park was not busy with people.

2. They happened between sunrise and 10:00 A.M.

3. They happened on mornings following an unusually cool night.

4. They happened when the lake was calm.

What is this spooky sound? Where does it come from? Perhaps we'll never know...unless the next story is the answer.

THE LAKE NEVER GIVES
UP ITS DEAD

Yellowstone Lake is not only the park's largest lake but one of the world's largest freshwater lakes as well. Geological evidence tells us that this mysterious lake may have at different times drained into the Pacific Ocean, the Arctic Ocean, and the Atlantic Ocean. The lake is 20 miles long, 14 miles wide, and has 110 miles of shoreline. The deepest point is 320 feet deep in the West Thumb area and the overall average depth is about 139 feet. Because of its altitude of 7,733 feet and the fact that it's fed by melting ice and snow, the lake stays an average of 41 degrees when it's not frozen.

The lake's low temperature makes it an extremely dangerous environment, especially when prevailing southwesterly winds produce waves five to six feet high. Many a soul has been lost in the lake.

Most people who have drowned in Yellowstone National Park have done so in Yellowstone Lake. There have been approximately forty drownings, mostly due to boating accidents. Once a boat swamps or overturns, there is little chance of survival. Victims have only about twenty minutes before hypothermia begins to set in. Death from the cold temperature is almost certain.

The first documented deaths were in 1894 when three men took a small rowboat on the lake on July 4th. The men headed for Stevenson Island with a supply of beer and plans to celebrate. When they didn't return that evening, a search began, but it was in vain. No one was found, just the little boat floating upside down near the shore of the island. The three bodies were never found.

Another drowning accident that took place prior to 1930 was just as mysterious, if not more so. In fact, the story ended up being rather bizarre and is most likely the very basis for the legend that Yellowstone Lake never gives up its dead.

The evening of August 26, 1906, started out like any other evening. A party of six young men and women set out in a small rowboat at West Thumb. Their destination? Nowhere in particular. They were just out to have an enjoyable time. Not more than one hundred yards from the shore, the small boat started to take on water. The weight of the six passengers was just too much and the rowboat started sinking. Panic struck and the passengers frantically started bailing, but the rowboat continued to fill. Soon it capsized and threw everyone into the icy water.

The two young women must have had the hardest time, as the bulkiness of their dresses and petticoats would have made it almost impossible to stay afloat. Against all odds and with all of her might, one of the ladies swam ashore.

One of the men, A.D. Taylor, with the aid of another male passenger whose name is not known, helped the second young lady. By this time the sun was down and the icy lake was becoming colder by the minute. It is not clear how, when, or in what condition the survivors were found, but only four made it through the disaster. W. B. Taylor, a brother of A.D. Taylor, and Harry Allen, an Army private stationed at Fort Yellowstone and assigned to the West Thumb soldier station, both lost their lives in the cold darkness of the lake that night. It's not certain if they died from hypothermia or drowning, but like those before them, their bodies were never found.

Here is where the legend comes in. The Taylor brothers were from Bozeman, Montana. About four months after the accident, Major Pitcher, the acting superintendent of Yellowstone National Park, received this somewhat odd letter from their father:

Bozeman, Mont
Dec 13th 1906
Maj Pitcher
Gardner Wyo

Dear Sir,
I write to you to know if you have ever learned anything from the two men drowned in Yellowstone Lake the 26th of August 1906. One of them was my son W. B. Taylor, the other one of the Soldier of the thumb, Allen by name. The reason why I ask is my son was a member of W O W & was insured. In that Long wishes us to write you to see if you have learned anything of them or not so you will please let me hear from you in regard to the matter. I have been told

by many that the lake never gives up its dead. If you know
this to be the case you will please make a statement to this
affect at your earliest convenience & oblige
  G P Taylor

Whatever were Major Pitcher's beliefs concerning
Yellowstone Lake, he was not at liberty to share it with
Mr. Taylor. It was true that a substantial number of
bodies drowned in the lake were never found. Major
Pitcher did, however, feel that the family of W. B. Taylor
needed reassurance of some kind. Why he chose to write
to Mrs. Taylor instead of Mr. Taylor is again a mystery,
but the letter was as follows:

Dec. 17 Th 6.
Mrs. G. P. Taylor,
Bozeman, Mont.

Dear Madam,
Replying to your letter of December 13th, I regret to
inform you that the bodies of the two men who were drowned
in Yellowstone Lake have not been recovered. Should the
body of your son ever be recovered, you will be promptly
notified. I am not able to state as to whether or not the
statement that the "lake never gives up its dead" is true.
  Yours respectfully,
  John Pitcher
  Major 6 Th Cavalry
  Acting Superintendent.

Strangely enough, park rangers who work on the lake have reported seeing what they thought were bodies floating to the surface or swept onto the shores. These bodies were said to be dressed in clothing of a century past. In fact, about a year after the Taylor accident, an employee of the lake's boat company discovered a human skull washed up on the west shore of Stevenson Island. Thinking that it might belong to W. B. Taylor, the family was notified as promised. Unfortunately the little flesh remaining on the jaws and skull, the left ear, and teeth were not enough to make a positive identification. Nevertheless, it was decided that it probably belonged to either Taylor or Allen. Later, other bones believed to be Allen's were also found and buried near the lakeshore.

Yellowstone Lake isn't the first lake to keep its dead. Lake Erie and several lochs in Europe are said to hold the same power. But why? There are several theories, both scientific and paranormal. Scientifically speaking, the lake is so cold that the bodies almost freeze, become heavy, and sink to the bottom.

Paranormally, most water deaths, because of the tragic nature of the accidents, make it difficult and even impossible sometimes for the spirit to move on. In this sense, even if the body is eventually found, the spirit remains trapped in the cold lake and does not move into the next world.

There is an old legend attached to "The Rhyme of the Ancient Mariner" which says that those who die at sea gather together to await judgment day. Perhaps the Whispers of Yellowstone Lake are really the voices of the drowned, beseeching the coming of their judgment day.

ABOUT THE AUTHOR

Shellie Herzog Larios has visited Yellowstone National Park practically every year since she was born. At Yellowstone, following her father's example, she learned to love nature. She also loved to hear and tell ghost stories, especially around a campfire, and she started reading and collecting ghost stories at a young age.

Larios served nearly 10 years in the U.S. Air Force and graduated from Weber (Utah) State University. She is married and has two children, who have shared many trips to Yellowstone with her.

Larios loves to investigate ghost stories from old and historic places. "Most people who live or work there always have a story," she says.

Larios pursues ghost stories from her home in Utah.